To Fire Warrior
and Peaceful Mind

Horse Song
The Naadam of Mongolia

Ted and Betsy Lewin

LEE & LOW BOOKS INC. *New York*

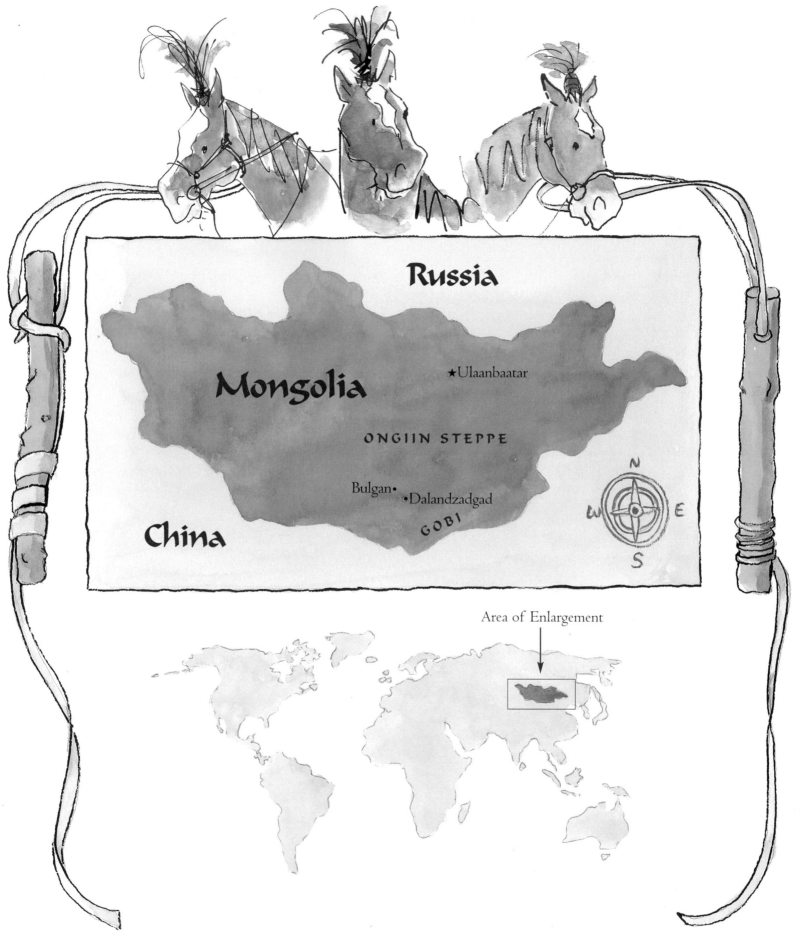

Bulgan is the name of a small town in southern Mongolia as well as a city and province in the north.

Mongolia!

Mongolia! This captivating land is one of the few unspoiled wilderness areas in the world. The landscape ranges from snow-capped mountains and dense forests to the wide-open steppe and the sandy soils of the Gobi. It is home to perhaps the last horse culture on Earth.

The people are warm and friendly. Out of a population of more than two and a half million, about one third lives in the capital of Ulaanbaatar. The rest are nomads who travel the vast countryside with their livestock and portable felt tent homes called *gers*. They carry with them only the most essential possessions, including richly ornamented everyday objects such as knives and saddles, and hand-carved and colorfully painted stools and tables.

Mongolian nomads and their horses are inseparable. "Never shout at your horse," people say. "It is your best friend." The horses are used for transportation and racing. They are small and have great strength and stamina, but are very uncomfortable to ride. To overcome this, riders often stand in the stirrups of their saddles while their horses trot. Riders need very strong leg muscles to do this.

Every summer Naadam festivals are held all around Mongolia to celebrate the country's most popular sports: wrestling, archery, and horse racing. The Naadam brings isolated nomads together to take part in the events, see friends and relatives, feast, and celebrate life. It is a time for Mongolians to remember centuries of tradition and keep their cultural heritage alive.

In the horse racing events, boys and girls race half-wild horses across the treeless steppe for honor and glory. It is these legendary child jockeys we have come so far to see.

Jack + Betsy

Arrival

"Are you Betsy and Ted?" asks a young woman as she steps from the crowd at the Ulaanbaatar airport. "I'm your guide. My name is Batsuren. It means 'fire warrior.' It's a boy's name. My mother consulted a shaman before I was born and was told I would be a boy." Batsuren laughs, then gestures to a giant of a man with a shaved head. "This is Amraa, our driver. Amraa means 'peaceful mind.'"

So off we go with Fire Warrior and Peaceful Mind on our great Mongolian adventure.

Our trip is eight hundred bumpy, roadless miles in a minivan. Along the way we encounter herds of horses, *hineks*, yaks, two-humped camels, and Mongolian "four-eyed" dogs.

We see nomads on horseback wearing long robes called *deels* and generals' hats called *janjins malgais*, and are astonished by throat singers playing horse-head fiddles. We find bones of dead horses, play dice games with sheep knuckles, and sleep in ger camps on the Ongiin steppe with crickets as big as cucumbers. We see black vultures with ten-foot wingspans. In the Gobi we marvel at the Flaming Cliffs, dense with dinosaur fossils.

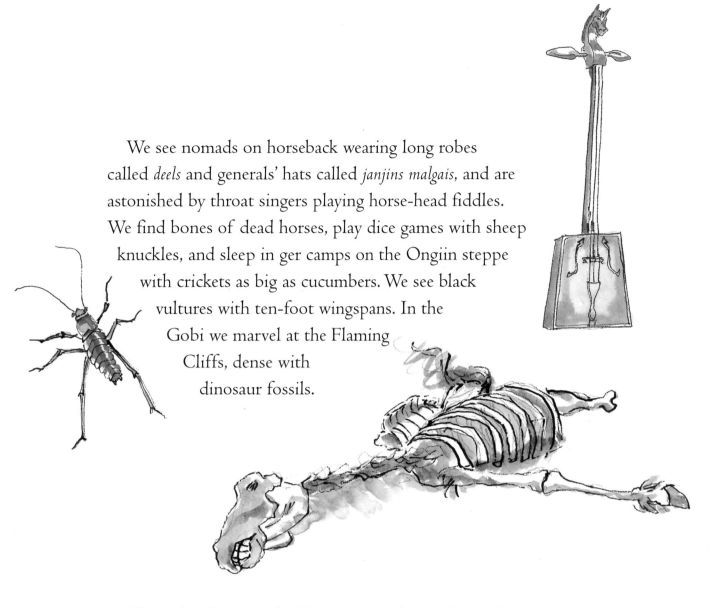

Three days later we finally reach our destination—the camp of the horse trainers.

Camp of the Horse Trainers

It is early morning on the steppe. We are awakened by mooing cows and bleating goats. As we crawl out of our little tent by the river, Amraa is fetching water and Batsuren is cooking breakfast. Suddenly we are surrounded by a large herd of horses that has come to the river to drink.

"Chu! Chu!" Batsuren yells, shooing away the horses. *"Chu! Chu!"*

There is stirring in the gers of the nomad family we are visiting. Grandma and Grandpa sleep in one ger, the rest of the family in another. The fires in the stoves are stoked, and everyone is getting ready for another long day.

Nine-year-old Tamir, home from boarding school in town for the summer break, has much to do before he can tend to his racehorse, the special one he will ride in the Naadam. He and the other children must milk the cows and goats, then drive them out to pasture. Tamir returns and leads some of the horses down to the river for watering.

The members of Tamir's family are some of the best horse
trainers in the country. They welcome us into their ger.

"*Sain bain uu,*" they say. "Hello."

"*Sain bain uu,*" we reply.

We're offered the traditional bowl of *airag,* a fermented drink made from mare's milk, plus a dish of curds and lumps of sugar. The airag tastes like watery, fizzy yogurt and smells faintly of horses.

Grandma is making fresh curds from the morning's milking of the cows and goats. The cheese-like curds are a staple of the family's diet. She slices them into squares with a long thread. Then they'll be dried in the sun on the roof of the ger.

We duck out through the low doorway of the ger to watch the catching of a horse that will be used for riding. A man rides out, standing up in the stirrups. He carries a ten-foot-long pole with a rope loop called an *uurag*. He plunges into the galloping herd, and with a lightning quick flip of the loop, snags a horse. The rider reins in his horse, pulling the lassoed horse up short. It is then

tethered at the *uya*, a long rope suspended like a clothesline between two poles.

The rider heads out into the herd again. This time the horses come straight at us. We don't know which way to go. Luckily the herd, now only a few feet away, veers sharply to the left just as the rider lassoes another horse.

During the summer the mares are milked every two hours. One of the older boys leads a foal to its mother and lets the young horse begin to nurse. After a few moments the foal is pulled away and some of the mare's milk is collected in a bucket. Then the foal is allowed to finish nursing.

We each take a turn churning the mare's milk in the big plastic drum. The milk must be churned a thousand times or more to start the fermentation that will turn it into airag. A new batch of airag is started every evening, and fresh milk is added throughout the day.

Out in front of the ger, Grandpa shows Tamir how to fix a bridle. We also talk about the stallions that will compete in the Naadam. Grandpa tells us a racehorse must have a narrow forehead, wide chest, flat back, and strong, slim legs. The racehorses receive special care starting months before the race. They are kept separated from the herd and tied at an uya. They are fed special grasses.

Like boys and girls everywhere in Mongolia, Tamir dreams of bringing honor, glory, and prizes to his family by winning the big race, now only one week away.

It's evening and time to "sweat up" the horses to get them in shape for the race. Tamir is given a leg up by his father and then rides in a circle to warm up his mount.

"Giiingoooo." In wailing, high-pitched voices, Tamir and the other young jockeys sing the traditional prerace song to encourage the horses. The jockeys then ride toward the horizon until they are almost out of sight.

Finally the horses turn. "Guriii!" the jockeys scream to make their horses run faster. "Guriiiii!" With their short wood-and-leather crops called *tashuurs*, the jockeys urge their horses to a full gallop. In a swirl of dust and thundering hooves, they race by us.

Near the gers the jockeys slow their horses to a walk and cool them down. The horses are tied up and the sweat is scraped from their coats with a long, flat stick called a *husuur*. Then the horses are groomed and watered.

At eleven o'clock at night the sun finally sets. The stars appear. The family is snug in its gers. Smoke drifts from the chimneys. We curl up in sleeping bags in our tent and listen to the river. Tomorrow the cows and goats must again be herded in for milking, the mares milked every two hours, and the racehorses sweated up and pampered.

The Day Before

It is the day before the Naadam. The jockeys, with their trainers, are camped in the hills surrounding the town where the Naadam is being held. Tamir's father is with us in the minivan.

We scan the hills, looking for Tamir's camp. His father worries about his son's ability to control the stallion. "Even though the name Tamir means 'strength,' the horse goes wherever it wants," his father says.

We stop at a camp to ask directions. We are welcomed by a group of men dressed in silk deels tied with long, colorful sashes. They invite us into a tiny, nylon tent.

"There's no room for us in there," we whisper to Batsuren.

"You must squeeze in," she replies. "It's a big honor to be invited."

So we squeeze in. The front opening is filled with curious onlookers. An old man offers us bowls of homemade liquor brewed from the milk of sheep, cows, and goats. It warms our stomachs, making us feel very much at home.

A little boy crawls into the tent. He is the jockey who will ride the old man's horse in the Naadam. The boy grins at us, puffing out his chest and showing off.

After two bowls of the warming drink, we reluctantly leave. We are still looking for the right camp. Soon Tamir's father spots it on a distant hillside.

We join Tamir's group and sit with the men and jockeys.
Curds, airag, and dried mutton are passed around. The jockeys
eat heartily and joke with one another. Tamir is quiet, though.
He is thinking about the big race.

After their meal the men tie the horses' tails, for decoration
and to keep the tails from getting in the way of other horses
when they race. The mounted jockeys then circle the campsite

singing *"Giiingoooo,"* and ride out across the steppe for one last
sweat up before the Naadam.

The jockeys and their trainers will spend the night at the horse
camp. We leave them at ten o'clock and return to the nearby
ger camp where we are staying. The sky is still bright blue and full
of billowing clouds as our minivan drives along. We pass lines of
mounted nomads, racehorses in tow, heading toward the town.

The Naadam

Amraa wakes us at four the next morning, and we arrive in town before sunrise. In the distance we hear the high-pitched strains of *"Giiingoooo"* as the jockeys sing to their horses and circle the uya. Their wailing makes our hair stand on end.

Soon groups of jockeys with their trainers gather in the rose-colored light of the rising sun. It is the first race of the day, Tamir's race.

The racers gather at the finish line. They will ride their horses at a walk fourteen miles across the Gobi to the starting line, then race back here. The trainers take the lead carrying *tugs*, long staffs topped with flowing white horsetails. The jockeys bunch up behind the leaders and the procession starts off, heading toward a distant mountain peak.

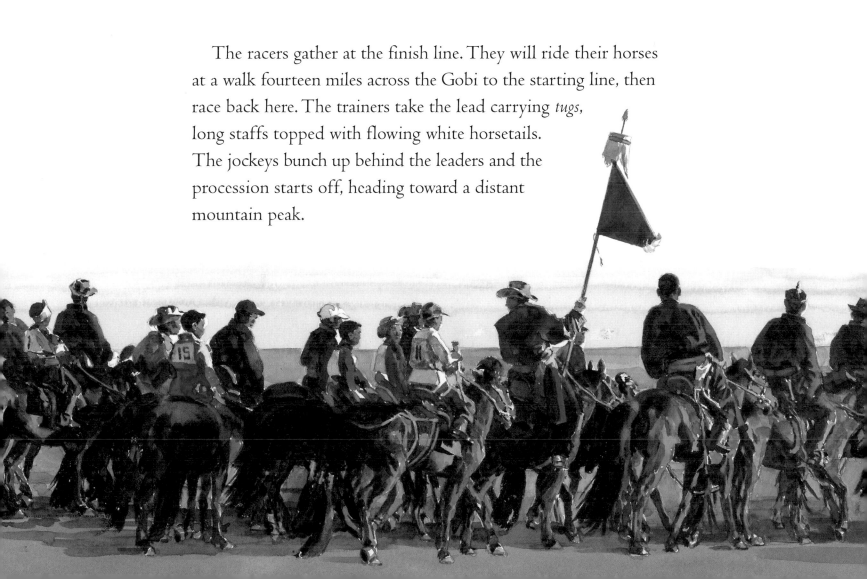

A jeep flying a big Mongolian flag brings up the rear of the group. The insistent *beep, beep, beep* of its horn herds the horses. Batsuren tells us that the man in the jeep with a bullhorn is yelling, "Keep in line! Go to the left! Keep up!"

We follow along in our minivan. The sun rises, bathing the
procession of brightly costumed riders in brilliant light. The riders
pass a herd of curious camels. Suddenly one of the horses bolts
forward and takes off. It's Tamir's horse! Tamir pulls on the
reins, struggling to control his mount.

"Keep in line," bellows the man with the bullhorn,
but Tamir disappears in the dust.

An hour later the jeep pulls ahead of the racers to a point fourteen miles from the finish line. A man holding a bright red flag jumps from the jeep, draws a line in the sand with the staff, and jams the flag into the ground. This is the starting line.

We wonder what's happened to Tamir.

In a cloud of dust we see the first horses approaching. To our
relief we spot Tamir in the middle of the pack. He's gotten control
of the stallion. The horses are supposed to come all the way to
the starting line and then go on a signal. But the minute the horses
see the red flag they know it's time to run. They bolt, turn, and
head back to the finish line. The jockeys cannot hold them.

Not one of the horses made it to the starting line.

The race has begun. **Pandemonium!**

"Guriii! GURIIIII!" The wild screams of the jockeys blend with the horses' shrill whinnies. The ground trembles and shakes as they race across the Gobi.

Dust envelops the little jockeys and their horses, and we can no longer see them. We run to our waiting minivan, where Amraa has Mongolian hip-hop music blaring from the radio. We slam the doors and buckle up. It's a rough, bumpy, zigzagging ride as we speed back to the finish line. We try to imagine what it must feel like to race at a full gallop on one of those half-wild horses.

Already the finish line is filled with nomads sitting on the ground, on horseback, and atop the finish line tower. The horses whinny and snort. The crowd is alive with excited anticipation.

Attendants on horseback hold colored wooden pegs painted with numbers. They will join the riders and take the horses' reins after they pass the finish line, giving each rider a peg to indicate his or her place: number one, number two, number three. . . .

We find a spot and sit on the ground behind the rope barrier.
Tamir's father joins us. All eyes are focused on the oncoming
cloud of dust.

The dust cloud gets larger and larger. Soon we see black specks floating in the heat shimmer. The specks magically become horses and riders. The crowd strains forward. The pounding of hooves grows louder as the lead horses and jockeys emerge. The stallions are at full gallop, lathered in sweat.

"GURIIIII! GURIIIII!" screams a jockey, flailing away with his tashuur. It's Tamir. The crowd goes wild as he crosses the finish line.

Tamir's father grins from ear to ear. His son has lived up to his name. His son has shown his strength. His son has won the race!

"He's number one!" we shout, proud to share this moment with the young horseman and his family.

Tamir's attendant rides alongside and takes the reins. More riders race out of the dust in groups of two, three, and four. On and on they come, until the last horse crosses the finish line.

"We call that horse the one with the wealthy stomach," says Batsuren, "because he's fat and out of shape."

The first race of the day is over.

There is great jubilation as Tamir rides into his camp. This horse has won races before. Last year's victory medal, tied to its forehead, glints in the sun.

Tamir is very serious, as all the young jockeys are. After dismounting he is given a ceremonial sip of airag by his father. Then Tamir poses for a winner's picture with his family, all dressed in their finest deels.

When the celebrating ends, Tamir walks around the camp with his hat over his face, acting silly like any nine-year-old!

The Closing Ceremony

The horses are here! Look, the horses!

The last race is over. The crowd surges forward to see the grand parade of winning horses and proud jockeys.

The jockeys circle the field twice, then line up facing the crowd. An elder, standing in the stirrups of his saddle, praises the horses with a "long rolling" song. He sings into a microphone, and the song booms from loudspeakers. The horses are decorated with medals, and the jockeys are kissed by the officials.

The owners of the horses are given ceremonial bowls of airag and their prizes—medals hanging from colorful ribbons, rugs,

and other traditional gifts. Nowadays, even nontraditional items such as television sets and motorbikes are sometimes included as prizes.

It's the end of the Naadam in this little Mongolian town. As the ceremonies come to a close, the young jockeys ride off on the horses that have brought them and their families so much honor and glory.

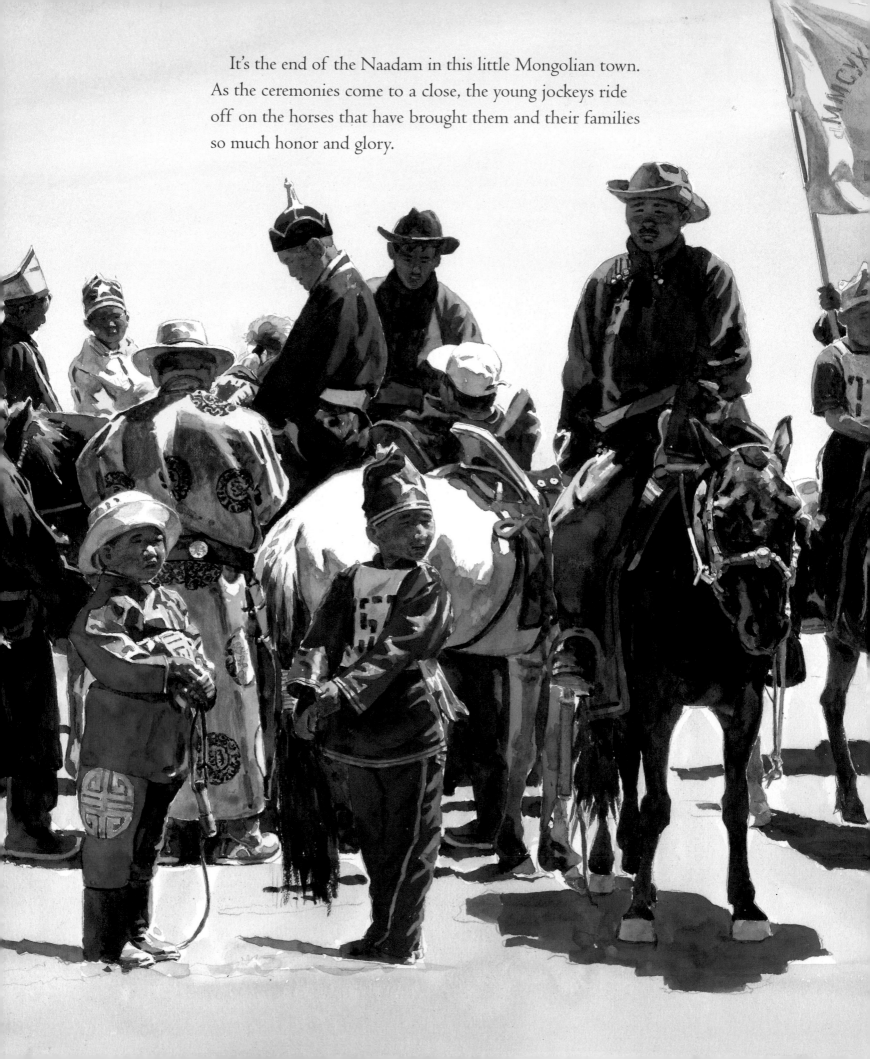

We close our eyes and hear for one last time their haunting horse song:

"Giiiingooooo-ooooo. Giingooo, giiiingoooooo!"

Ger Facts

A ger is a collapsible round tent made of wood and felt. It has kept its original form for centuries. The outside binding of horsehair holds up the whole thing. The lower half is a latticelike wall made of willow wood that folds together. A ger stays warm in winter and cool in summer.

The roof ring at the top of a ger represents the heavens. The radiating roof poles represent the rays of the sun. The two supporting poles represent the mother and the father. Never step between them!

The roof ring also acts as a natural sundial. The slant of the sun's rays indicates the time for milking and pasturing. If light rays reach to the back of the ger, it's too late to set out on a long journey.

Announcing oneself is not necessary when entering a ger. Don't step on the threshold. It's bad luck. Enter, go left, and sit on the floor, feet facing the door. Always accept the airag with both hands and taste it. Try the curds and lumps of sugar you are offered.

All ger doors face south. Originally the doors were felt flaps. The decorated, wooden doors of today are a Russian introduction. The door can be locked, but this goes against traditional hospitality.

On the north side of the ger a cupboard holds family photos and religious items. East is the women's side, with a bed and kitchen. West is the men's side and everyone else's. All the horse gear is on the west side too. Usually the wife gets the bed and everybody else sleeps on the floor.

Traditionally there was no stove and chimney in a ger. Smoke from the fire pit escaped through an opening at the top. The rising smoke permeated the felt covering, making it waterproof. Today a chimney carries away the smoke from the stove, so plastic is placed between the felt and canvas coverings to keep the ger dry inside. More and more, a TV screen flickers inside and a motorbike sits outside the ger.

A ger must be broken down and fit onto one camel when a family moves from one location to another. Today some families transport their gers in a truck, even though gasoline is not always easy to come by.

When setting up a ger in a new location, the pieces of furniture that won't fit through the door are arranged on the ground. The ger is then put up around them.

Japanese architects visited Mongolia to study the design of the ger to see if they could improve on it. They couldn't.

Other Mongolia Facts

There are twice as many horses in Mongolia as there are people. In a year when rain and food are plentiful, there could be up to three times as many horses as people.

The Mongolian word for horse is *mur.* There are four hundred words to describe a horse's characteristics, with one hundred eighty words to describe its color. Horses are never given human names.

If you don't like the road you're driving on in the countryside, you can make another one alongside it.

Among Mongolians it is impolite to point your finger at people. If you do so accidentally, bring the rest of your fingers up so it appears you are gesturing with your whole hand.

When Mongolians give directions, they point in one of three ways. A straight finger means "far away in that direction," a one-quarter bent finger means "not quite so far away," and a half-bent finger means "fairly close." Even if the person asking directions knows the other person is wrong, he or she listens very attentively until the direction giver is finished.

The Naadam is held each summer from July 11 to 13 in many locations around the country. The festival dates back almost one thousand years and is the world's second oldest sporting event, after the Olympics.

Several different games are played using sheep knuckles as dice. Depending on which side they fall, the dice represent one of four animals: horse, camel, sheep, or goat. The horse side is the most desirable, the sheep side next, then the camel, and last the goat.

Mongolians like to solve puzzles made of metal wire, wood, bones, or other materials. A puzzle is also used to test a prospective bride. If she can solve the puzzle, she'll be able to solve any problem that might arise.

If you accidentally step on someone's foot, you shake hands.

In Mongolian there are many commands to animals that mean "Go": *Chu!* (horse), *Jov!* (dog), *Cha!* (sheep), *Huj!* (cow).

Glossary and Pronunciation Guide

airag (AIR-ig) beverage made of fermented mare's milk

Amraa (AHM-rah) Mongolian name meaning "peaceful mind"

Batsuren (bat-SOR-en) Mongolian name meaning "fire warrior"

cha (chah) go, when commanding a sheep

chu (choo) go, when commanding a horse

curd (kerd) thick part of milk that separates from the watery part when milk sours

deel (dell) long garment overlapped in the front and tied with a sash

ferment (fer-MENT) undergo a gradual chemical change caused by bacteria, yeast, etc.

fermentation (fer-men-TAY-shen) act or process of fermenting

foal (fohl) young horse, especially less than one year old

ger (gair) collapsible round tent with wooden frame and felt covering

gingo (GING-goh) traditional prerace song sung by jockeys at a Naadam festival

Gobi (GOH-bee) desert in eastern Asia, mostly in southern Mongolia

Guri (gor-EE) Mongolian deity, or god, protector of horses; racers call to Guri to make their horses run faster

hinek (HI-nek) animal that is a cross between a yak and a cow

huj (oodch) go, when commanding a cow

husuur (who-SOOR) long, flat stick used to scrape sweat from a horse

janjin (jan-GIN) general

jockey (JAH-kee) person who rides a horse in a race

jov (jove) go, when commanding a dog

malgai (MAL-guy) hat

mare (mair) adult female horse

mur (mer) horse; the Mongolian horse has a stocky build and relatively short legs

Naadam (NAH-dum) Mongolian national summer festival with wrestling, archery, and horse racing events

nomad (NOH-mad) member of a group that moves from place to place

Ongiin steppe (on-JEEN step) plain in the mid-eastern part of Mongolia

pandemonium (pan-deh-MOH-nee-um) wild uproar or confusion

sain bain uu (sine bah NOO) hello

shaman (SHAH-men) person who is believed to have close contact with the spirit world

stallion (STAL-yen) adult male horse

steppe (step) vast, treeless, grass-covered plain

stirrup (STER-up) ring that hangs from the side of a saddle to support a rider's foot

Tamir (TAH-mir) Mongolian name meaning "strength"

tashuur (TASH-oor) short wood-and-leather whip used when riding a horse

tug (tugh) long staff topped with a white horsetail

Ulaanbaatar (OO-lan-BAH-tar) capital of Mongolia

uurag (OO-rog) long herding pole with a lasso at the end

uya (OO-yah) long rope suspended between two poles

yak (yak) large, long-haired ox

Acknowledgments

Special thanks to Gereltuv Dashdoorov and Nomadic Expeditions.

This story is based on actual events that took place in 2004 in Dalandzadgad and Bulgan, in southern Mongolia. Tamir is a composite of several young jockeys we met on our trip.

The illustration on the half-title page is a representation of a painted ger door.

LEE & LOW BOOKS Inc., 95 Madison Avenue, New York, NY 10016
leeandlow.com

Manufactured in China
Book design by Tania Garcia
Book production by The Kids at Our House
The text is set in Centaur
The full-color illustrations are rendered in watercolor on Strathmore bristol board. The spot illustrations are rendered in reed pen and watercolor, also on Strathmore bristol board.

10 9 8 7 6 5 4 3 2
First Edition

Library of Congress Cataloging-in-Publication Data

Lewin, Ted.
Horse song : the Naadam of Mongolia / Ted and Betsy Lewin. — Ist ed.
p. cm.
Summary: "Ted and Betsy Lewin describe the landscapes, people, and activities they encounter during a trip to Mongolia for Naadam, the annual summer festival where child jockeys ride half-wild horses for miles across the Mongolian steppe"—Provided by publisher.
ISBN 978-1-58430-277-3
1. Summer festivals—Mongolia. 2. Mongolia—Social life and customs.
I. Lewin, Betsy. II. Title.
GT4505.81.M65L49 2008
306.0951'.7—dc22
2007025899